MYSTERIES UNWRAPPED:
HAUNTED U.S.A.

WRITTEN BY
CHARLES WETZEL

ILLUSTRATED BY
JOSH COCHRAN

STERLING

New York / London
www.sterlingpublishing.com/kids

STERLING and the distinctive Sterling logo are registered trademarks of
Sterling Publishing Co., Inc.

Library of Congress Cataloging-in-Publication Data Available

10 9 8 7 6 5 4 3 2 1

Published by Sterling Publishing Co., Inc.
387 Park Avenue South, New York, NY 10016

Text © 2008 by Charles Wetzel
Illustrations © 2008 by Josh Cochran
Distributed in Canada by Sterling Publishing
c/o Canadian Manda Group, 165 Dufferin Street
Toronto, Ontario, Canada M6K 3H6
Distributed in the United Kingdom by GMC Distribution Services
Castle Place, 166 High Street, Lewes, East Sussex, England BN7 1XU
Distributed in Australia by Capricorn Link (Australia) Pty. Ltd.
P.O. Box 704, Windsor, NSW 2756, Australia

Printed in China
All rights reserved

Sterling ISBN 978-1-4027-3735-0

Book design by Joshua Moore of beardandglasses.com

For information about custom editions, special sales, premium and
corporate purchases, please contact Sterling Special Sales
Department at 800-805-5489 or specialsales@sterlingpublishing.com.

IT IS WONDERFUL THAT
FIVE THOUSAND YEARS HAVE
NOW ELAPSED SINCE THE
CREATION OF THE WORLD,
AND STILL IT IS UNDECIDED
WHETHER OR NOT THERE HAS
EVER BEEN AN INSTANCE OF
THE SPIRIT OF ANY PERSON
APPEARING AFTER DEATH.
ALL ARGUMENT IS AGAINST IT;
BUT ALL BELIEF IS FOR IT.
-- SAMUEL JOHNSON

CONTENTS

In 2005, Gary Evans was driving past the cemetery on Watts Road in Watts Mill, South Carolina, when a movement caught his eye.

Could it be? he wondered.

No, of course not. But there she was.

Walking through the graveyard, close to the road, was a young woman with long hair. "She had good features [and] a well-defined body," Gary wrote, "[though I] could not actually see her face well enough to describe her, she was wearing a dress that was form fitting and dated. It reminded me of a dress that women would have worn in the late 1800s."

Gary stopped his truck, got out, and pointed a bright flashlight at her.

"I could see her just fine and would guess she was about forty or fifty feet in front of me. As my light panned toward her, she totally disappeared."

This was Gary's second encounter with the woman in white; the first time he watched her for about thirty seconds before getting back into his truck and leaving. He still passes the cemetery and keeps an eye out, hoping for another glimpse of this attractive but insubstantial figure.

Gary's experience is not unique. From Canada to Mexico and coast to coast, people regularly encounter ghosts, specters, and wraiths of every description. They are America's phantom population, the native citizens of Haunted U.S.A.

INTRODUCTION

Our search for Haunted U.S.A. begins with "the house."

There's no need to describe the house; you can see it in your imagination: the empty boarded-up place with blank windows, peeling paint, and a weed-choked yard. It can be found almost anywhere: standing at the edge of a cornfield, by the railroad tracks, in a city, or even at the end of your block. Little kids run past it when the sun is up and stay away after dark. Older ones have things to prove and dare one another to knock on the door.

Darers go first.

It's the murder house, the place where someone committed suicide or died in a terrible accident. People tell stories about it. Maybe a face has been seen staring out the attic window, or a woman in a bustle walks in the ruined garden and vanishes when spoken to. Perhaps there is a permanent bloodstain on the bedroom floor.

A guy at school told me that his brother's friend snuck in one night to see it, and when he came out his hair was white! He never spoke a word after that but screamed all night, and his parents had to put him in the state mental hospital.

Sometimes it's not a house, but a cemetery, an abandoned church, a dark stretch of road, or a rusty bridge.

Yeah, this carload of kids was on their way to the prom around 1985, I guess. Anyway, it was a foggy night, and they smashed right into the bridge. When the police got there, they found three of 'em dead, but the fourth never turned up. Guess she went into the river 'cause nights when the fog's thick, folks have seen a pretty blond girl all dressed up standing by the bridge.

The horror novelist Stephen King once wrote that the truest definition of a haunted house is a house with an "unsavory history," and the same seems to apply to forests, schools, and theaters. But does that mean we can find haunted places with a formula? Something like Age + Tragedy and/or Violence = Spooks.

Judging by how hauntings are portrayed in both traditional and popular form, many people seem to believe it works just this way. But has anyone told the ghosts? It's certainly something to consider as we move forward in our search for Haunted America, and where better to begin than with an American house that offers a combination of fame, history, and celebrity ghosts—as well as ongoing paranormal phenomena that are unrivaled.

1. AMERICA'S MOST HAUNTED HOUSES

GHOSTS IN THE WHITE HOUSE

The president of the United States lives in a mansion built in the early 1800s. This house is instantly recognizable to most Americans, but what they may not know is that it is one of the most haunted houses in the country.

The first residents of this famous mansion were second president John Adams and his wife, Abigail. While Mr. Adams ran the country, Mrs. Adams ran the house. And one of her daily chores can still be seen today. Witnesses report seeing the spirit of Abigail Adams hanging laundry in the East Room, a vision often said to be accompanied by the smell of soap and wet laundry.

A few years after the Adamses moved out, fourth president James Madison and his wife, Dolley, took up residence in the White House. They were still there when the mansion was burned by British invaders during the War of 1812. Although the house was rebuilt, there are two scorch marks on the building that serve as reminders of the war. But there's another reminder as well: the apparition of a British soldier carrying a lit torch has frequently been seen on the White House's front lawn. The ghost presumably dates from 1814, when the mansion was set on fire.

Other strange phenomena have been reported in the mansion as well, including mysterious voices, footsteps, lamps turning themselves off and on in the family quarters, and apparitions. After all, it is not only war that creates ghosts. Over the years, the White House has been the scene of death, grief, madness, and decisions that have changed the course of history. Some of the most important decisions were made by Abraham Lincoln, whose eleven-year-old son, Willie, was among the first specters to take up residence in the house.

When Willie died of typhoid in 1862, his parents were grief-stricken; Mrs. Lincoln tried communicating with him through séances and claimed that his spirit often stood at the foot of her bed. These visions could easily be dismissed as those of a grieving parent if not for a housekeeper's report in later years that the White House staff had been frightened by the appearance of a phantom boy. Willie's ghost was frequently seen during the Grant administration, most often in the second-floor bedrooms. His footsteps were heard in the room where he died, and Lyndon Johnson's daughter, Lynda, is said to have had some kind of encounter with the boy.

Like his son, Abraham Lincoln has also been seen or sensed throughout the house. Many people, including important visitors, presidential family members, and White House personnel such as Tony Savoy, former White House operations foreman, have reported sightings. According to Savoy, he was watering the plants one morning when he saw Mr. Lincoln dressed in a grey pinstriped suit. The ghost was sitting in a chair with his long legs crossed, but when Savoy blinked, the figure disappeared. During

President Franklin Delano Roosevelt's long administration, a White House clerk claimed to see Mr. Lincoln sitting on a bed, taking his boots off. More recently, President Ronald Reagan's daughter, Maureen, and her husband allegedly saw apparitions in the Lincoln Bedroom, including Lincoln himself, standing by the fireplace. The sixteenth president's lanky shape has been seen crossing hallways and in his former office, the Cabinet Room, and the Lincoln Bedroom, where it is said that First Lady Eleanor Roosevelt often felt like someone was watching her.

Tales of former presidents still in residence are not uncommon. Mary Lincoln claimed to have heard Andrew Jackson stomping around the Rose Room using terrible language and reported seeing John Tyler proposing to his wife in the Yellow Oval Room. Stories have also been told of President William Henry Harrison rummaging through boxes in the house's attic, though what he was looking for, no one knows.

More than just the president's family live in the White House. America's most famous building is also home to a number of ghostly beings. (COURTESY LIBRARY OF CONGRESS)

OLD HICKORY VS. OLD KATE

Andrew Jackson was called "Old Hickory" because he was as tough as hickory wood. His ferocity was legendary; he won the Battle of New Orleans, drove the Spanish and the Seminole Indians from Florida, fought duels, and, as the seventh president of the United States, regretted that he could not shoot or hang his political opponents. According to legend, Jackson met his match in the Bell Witch, a poltergeist also known as "Old Kate." The Bell Witch had spent years plaguing the Bell family of Tennessee, yanking sheets off beds, slapping members of the family, and being exceptionally rude to everyone. In 1819, the general decided to see it for himself.

On the way there, his wagon stopped and would not proceed until Jackson admitted that the spirit was responsible. Jackson was accompanied by a sort of exorcist, who announced that he planned to "kill" the ghost but never got a chance; Old Kate seized the would-be ghost-killer and beat him into submission.

Jackson left the next day and swore that he would rather face the whole British army than tackle the Bell Witch again.

Many White House ghost stories have become tall tales, such as Dolley Madison's ghost appearing in the Rose Garden to prevent First Lady Edith Wilson from digging up the flowers, but then there's the kind of experience described by former Chief Usher Gary Walters. Walters claims that he was with three police officers when they felt a cool breeze and saw a double-door close by itself. "I have never seen these doors move before without somebody specifically closing them by hand," Mr. Walters wrote. "It was quite remarkable."

4

THE MORRIS-JUMEL MANSION

In 1964, a group of noisy schoolchildren were taking a tour of New York City's Morris-Jumel Mansion when an old woman appeared on a balcony and yelled at them to be quiet; she was later identified as the former owner, Eliza Jumel, who died in 1865.

Eliza's wealthy husband, Stephen, was killed in a mysterious pitchfork accident in 1832, and the rich widow immediately married Aaron Burr, the seventy-seven-year-old ex–vice president of the United States. The marriage was not a happy one, and she began divorce proceedings soon after the wedding; it was granted on the day Burr died. Eliza spent the rest of her long life alone, and possibly insane, inside the mansion. Her ghost wears a purple dress, raps on the walls, and haunts the house along with a servant girl and a Revolutionary War soldier. The spirits of Stephen Jumel and Aaron Burr are also said to have made appearances at the house.

THE CAPITOL IS HAUNTED

The residence at 1600 Pennsylvania Avenue might be America's Haunted House, but Washington, D.C., is thick with history, and others are close by. Just one block west of the White House lies a handsome brick building that has six sides, yet is known as the "Octagon House."

Although President James Madison was the house's most famous resident (he lived there after the White House was destroyed), it was also the home of the Tayloe family. According to legend, Colonel Tayloe discovered that his daughter was involved with a young British officer, whom he refused to let her marry. After a terrific argument, she climbed to the top of the house's winding staircase and fell three stories to her death. Improbable as it sounds, the same thing is supposed to have happened to her sister, only this Tayloe girl eloped, returned home to beg forgiveness, and then went over the railing and died.

The Octagon House is said to be haunted by the sound of footsteps on the stairs, followed by a scream and a crash, plus an occasional apparition climbing the stairs. Footsteps are also heard on the third floor, a shadow is seen on the spot where the second Tayloe girl fell to her death, and the smell of Dolley Madison's lilac perfume sometimes fills the rooms. In the early 1960s, the Octagon House's superintendent, Alric H. Clay, repeatedly found all the lights turned on and a door to which he had the only key unlocked. Today the building is the headquarters of the American Institute of Architects, though it can't be easy to concentrate on blueprints with all those distractions.

Two blocks north and one block east of the Octagon House is another brick building that was once the home of Commodore Stephen Decatur. Decatur is remembered today for his naval expeditions against the Barbary Pirates and the British. He was a national hero when he and his wife moved into the house in 1818. Just two years later, he died there after being shot in a duel. A military-looking figure, presumably Decatur, has been seen standing at the windows, particularly the downstairs bedroom window, which is now bricked up. The figure has also been spotted walking out the front door and into Lafayette Square.

Washington, D.C.'s Octagon House has reportedly been the sight of many tragedies—and many hauntings. (COURTESY LIBRARY OF CONGRESS)

LONG BEFORE BECOMING
SUPERNATURAL HIMSELF,
THE COMMODORE HAD HIS
OWN ENCOUNTER WITH
SOMETHING STRANGER
THAN A GHOST.

Long before becoming supernatural himself, the commodore had his own encounter with something stranger than a ghost. According to legend, Decatur was firing cannons at the Hanover Iron Works in Hanover, New Jersey, when a dragon-like creature with leathery wings and a head like a horse came flapping out of the woods. It was the notorious Jersey Devil. Decatur, who had faced pirates and British warships, did not panic. He took aim, fired, and punched a hole clear through the thing's body. The fiend, undisturbed, flew back into the forest.

Unlikely as it sounds, Washington, D.C., has a phantom monster of its own. It prowls the halls of Congress at night, appearing near the Crypt, a tomb built for George Washington but never used. Witnesses describe an ordinary-looking black cat that pads toward them out of the shadows and then does something unexpected. The cat undergoes a rapid change, swelling up like an emergency life raft until an elephant-sized feline fills the corridor. People who find themselves dwarfed by the Demon Cat say that they suddenly know how a mouse or sparrow feels. In fact, one elderly guard was so terrified that his heart stopped.

No one knows where the Demon Cat came from, but sightings are said to occur before a change in government, a national disaster, or other major catastrophes. Whatever the case, the Demon Cat is certainly the most terrifying and bizarre specter in a very haunted city.

THE WHALEY HOUSE

California's Whaley House is on everyone's "most haunted" list. In 1863, Thomas Whaley built the first brick house in San Diego as a general store, granary, and home for his family. It stands on the site of a botched execution, the hanging of a thief called "Yankee Jim" Robinson.

At first things went well for Whaley. He was successful in business and became a prominent member of the community. But then came financial and political reverses that included a mob breaking into his home. Whaley's family was plagued with illness, death, and insanity. All of these seem to have left their mark. Reported hauntings at the Whaley House include phantom footsteps, organ music, and a rocking chair that moves under its own power. Witnesses have also described seeing Mr. Whaley wearing a frock coat in the parlor; a small dark woman wearing a print dress, cap, and gold hoop earrings; and the Whaleys' dog, a terrier named Dolly Varden. The main phenomenon, however, seems to be unexplained smells, including lavender, food cooking, and cigar smoke.

THE WINCHESTER MYSTERY HOUSE

Houses throughout the world are built with charms, amulets, and supernatural barriers designed to keep out malevolent spirits. Chinese homes, for example, once included "ghost walls," or screens, which are found inside the gates of houses and are decorated with pictures of gods and symbols to drive away evil influences. In Thailand, elaborately decorated miniature houses called *sarn phra phum* are everywhere. People encourage the spirits to live in them, rather than their own homes. The houses are even equipped with little ceramic servants, a horse, and an elephant for the spirit's convenience.

American architects, in contrast, seldom design with the supernatural in mind. If a house becomes haunted, it's assumed to be the result of a bad site (such as the Whaley House), or because something terrible happened on the premises. There have been a few homes, however, designed to prevent spirits from lurking.

When it comes to building with ghosts in mind, the Winchester Mystery House in San Jose, California, is unrivaled ...maybe. The house's biggest mystery is why Sarah Winchester insisted that the mansion be constantly expanded and altered by a team of carpenters and craftsmen working twenty-four hours a day, seven days a week for thirty-eight years. In fact, the only break during this time was just after the earthquake of 1906; it was still under construction when she died in 1922. Sarah inherited the Winchester Rifle fortune when her husband died and spent millions on her strange project, but she never explained why. It's believed that she held séances and that the spirits she spoke with gave her building instructions. Other stories claim that Sarah was told she would die if she ever stopped building. It is also rumored that the house was intended either to shelter the souls of those killed by Winchester rifles or as a place where the widow could hide from their vengeful ghosts. Although there is no hard proof to support either claim, there are several reasons for thinking the second explanation might be true.

First, Mrs. Winchester had forty bedrooms and slept in a different one every night—certainly the behavior of someone trying to hide. Second, the house's layout is an incredibly confusing maze of about 160 rooms—some of which are completely

The Winchester Mystery House in San Jose, California, spans over four acres. To this day, no one knows why Sarah Winchester decided to build it.
(© WINCHESTER MYSTERY HOUSE, SAN JOSE, CA)

enclosed by other rooms. There are secret passages, a bell tower, stairs going up to the ceiling, chimneys without fireplaces, closets that are entrances to rooms, doors that open onto blank walls or steep drops, and halls that double back to where they started.

Moreover, in a world of people who dislike the number thirteen, Sarah Winchester used it at every opportunity. Stairs have thirteen steps, rooms thirteen windows, windows thirteen panes, doors thirteen panels, and if a chandelier did not have thirteen branches, more were added. Even the drains have thirteen holes! Sarah was also fond of ornamental daisies and spider webs, and these appear throughout the building.

Some people claim the mansion is haunted, pointing to stories of unexplained voices, cold spots, banging doors, and doorknobs moving themselves, while others say that a place so big and oddly laid out is bound to produce unexpected echoes, breezes, and shadows. Tour guides, however, claim to have seen a man in overalls who resembles one of Mrs. Winchester's longtime carpenters. Who knows what might be lurking in its dusty forgotten rooms?

THE TRAPEZIUM HOUSE

The Trapezium House is a three-story brick house in Petersburg, Virginia, that was built in 1817 by an Irish immigrant named Charles O'Hara. According to legend, O'Hara's West Indian servant told him that evil spirits hide in right angles, so the house was built without them; not a single ninety-degree angle can be found in its floors, stairs, walls, or windows. Evil spirits had no place to roost, which O'Hara made especially certain of by burning candles all night.

The Amityville house where six members of the DeFeo family were shot to death in 1974 is said to be the sight of numerous ghostly occurrences. (© BETTMANN/CORBIS)

THE MOST FAMOUS HAUNTED HOUSE THAT NEVER WAS

There's an ordinary looking suburban house in Amityville, Long Island, with a horrific history. On the night of November 13, 1974, six members of the DeFeo family were shot dead by the oldest son, twenty-four-year-old Ronald DeFeo Jr.

A year after the massacre, the Lutz family moved into the house, which the previous owner had christened "High Hopes." They left four weeks later. During that time, they claim to have undergone a terrifying haunting. Author Jay Anson took their account and turned it into a wildly popular nonfiction book called *The Amityville Horror* (1977), which led to a series of movies that continue today.

The Lutzes described cold spots, smells, voices, the feeling of invisible hands, object-movement, and levitation, as well as clouds of flies, phantom marching bands, green slime oozing out of the walls, demonic figures, and "Jodie," a giant floating pig with glowing red-eyes.

The Amityville Horror is said to be a true story, but one researcher claimed to find more than 100 factual errors in a book just 256 pages long. Ronald DeFeo Jr.'s lawyer maintains that he invented the story with George Lutz, and it was then given to Jay Anson who dramatized it and used his imagination to fill in the blanks. Anson was honest; he did not believe in the paranormal. He just wanted to write a bestseller that would make him enough money to retire.

Several families have lived in the house since the Lutzes left, but they've reported nothing stranger than sightseers and odd people showing up at their door. Even these unwelcome visitors are now rare, since the house's address and appearance were changed. The quarter-circle windows that once stared off countless book covers like evil eyes are now a pair of ordinary rectangles. For all its fame, it seems that the Amityville Horror may have been no more than a hoax.

2.

THESE
HONORED DEAD

The Civil War almost destroyed the United States. When the fighting ended, some 620,000 soldiers were dead and countless roads, fields, buildings, and bridges had been the scenes of terrible violence, which seems to have left a supernatural mark. There might be more ghosts connected to the Civil War than any other single event in American history, and the most haunted place of all may well be a small town that few had heard of before the war.

GETTYSBURG

Gettysburg was the turning point of the Civil War, the beginning of the end for the South, and the bloodiest battle ever fought on American soil. In 1863, the Confederate army under Robert E. Lee invaded the Union. When Lee's Army of Northern Virginia encountered George G. Meade's forces at the Pennsylvania town of Gettysburg, a titanic battle erupted. The troops fought from July first to July third, and when the smoke cleared, General Lee had been defeated.

As many as 8,000 men were dead, and 26,000 more wounded, captured, or missing. Bodies of men and horses lay in stinking mounds or strewn through the town and green summer fields. If the popular belief that hauntings are caused by violence and suffering is true, then Gettysburg must be one of the most haunted places in the United States; and it seems to be just that. In fact, the first ghost appeared during the battle itself.

The 20th Maine Volunteer Infantry Regiment had been ordered to take a hill called the "Little Round Top," but they couldn't find it. Suddenly a man riding a magnificent white horse and wearing a three-cornered hat appeared. He drew his sword and led the way to the hill, where the Mainers held a crucial position during the battle. The identity of the man on horseback was never in doubt; George Washington, dead since 1799, had returned from the grave to help save the country. A terrific battle took place on the Little Round Top, and to this day the hill is haunted by a headless horseman, presumably not Washington, but rather a Union officer decapitated by a cannonball.

But the headless horseman is far from Gettysburg's only ghost. Spectral troops appear all over the battlefield. During the fighting, Texas sharpshooters climbed onto a pile of massive boulders called the Devil's Den and picked off men on the Little Round Top. Scruffy, rifle-toting phantoms have been appearing there ever since. Not all of the ghosts are in the countryside, either. Much of the fighting took place in town, and when the battle was over, every building was turned into a hospital—or morgue—which might explain what happened to two people who worked at Gettysburg College.

One night they were taking the elevator down when it missed their floor and continued on to the basement. The doors slid open, and the passengers found themselves looking at a nineteenth-century vision of horror. There were rows of beds containing

THE IDENTITY OF THE MAN
ON HORSEBACK WAS NEVER
IN DOUBT; GEORGE
WASHINGTON, DEAD SINCE
1799, HAD RETURNED FROM
THE GRAVE TO HELP SAVE
THE COUNTRY.

wounded and mutilated men, and, even worse, a bloodstained doctor stood by an operating table surrounded by piles of freshly amputated limbs. The doctor looked at the two in the elevator and began moving toward them when—mercifully—the door closed and the car began going up again, taking them to the right floor and century.

An even more extraordinary apparition occurs annually near the Maryland border, along Route 116, on the nights of July fourth and fifth. Witnesses claim that a faint moaning sound is heard. The noise grows louder, and soon a line of phantom horse-drawn wagons comes lumbering along. They are loaded with wounded Confederates, and the air is filled with awful sobs and moans of injured men being roughly bounced along the road. Tired soldiers escort the convoy, and then the whole scene, a reenactment of Lee's retreat to the Potomac, evaporates.

HUPP'S HILL

Gettysburg has long attracted tourists and reenactors (men and women who wear period clothing, carry antique rifles, and are probably responsible for more than one sighting), but the last few years have seen it become *the* favorite destination for ghost hunters. The battlefield park is such an enormous place—almost four thousand acres—that the footsore ghost hunter might consider visiting another spot: Hupp's Hill in Strasburg, Virginia.

During the Civil War, Hupp's Hill overlooked the only all-weather road through the Shenandoah Valley. Both sides held the hill at different times, but the Union fortified it with trenches and earthworks—mounds of earth built to protect the soldiers—and was able to fire on Confederates moving on the turnpike below. It was the scene of deadly fighting and may even contain a mass grave, but today it is an historic park. If there's any place in the United States that can be called *hyperhaunted* it is Hupp's Hill, where a haunted museum stands on a haunted battlefield over a haunted cave.

At the top of the hill is the Stonewall Jackson Museum. Unexplained lights have been seen coming from the attic

The Stonewall Jackson Museum makes up the top layer of a multilayered haunted hotspot. (© RICHARD T. NOWITZ/CORBIS)

windows between two and three in the morning, and objects are routinely moved. A Confederate hospital bed once displayed with a heavy woolen blanket is now kept bare because the blanket refused to stay in one place. There's also a nineteenth-century black dress that won't stay on the hanger, possibly because the original owner is trying to get it back; a filmmaker who visited the museum snapped a picture of the dress along with what looked like a skeleton seated next to it. Ghosts even browse the gift shop, where staff members have arrived in the morning to find little boxes of souvenirs stacked up on the counter.

The museum is full of supernatural activity, but if you want to see apparitions it's better to be outside on the battlefield. Spectral soldiers and officers have been reported all over the hill, with sightings by the flagpole, inside one of the big sinkholes (a depression in the ground caused by erosion), and on the earthworks. The most distinctive ghost is a Union drummer boy that appeared to multiple witnesses during the Battlefield Lantern Tour in October of 2000; it's believed that his body is buried nearby. Ghost hunters investigating the Civil War Trail also discovered a mysterious cold spot in the woods. But even odder things happen *under* the battlefield.

Crystal Caverns is small by the standards of more famous caves, but it has a rich history. At various times it has been used as a hospital, prison, speakeasy, and dance hall. Jeane Dixon, a famous clairvoyant who some say predicted the assassination of President John F. Kennedy, was a frequent visitor because she believed the crystals sharpened her psychic powers.

The ghosts of several Native Americans and Civil War soldiers are said to haunt the cave, but its best-known residents are Emily and the Major. Emily was a little girl who died sometime in the early nineteenth century. Psychics claim she wandered away from a Fourth of July fireworks display and went down into the cave with a lantern or candle. She was found there several days later, dead from exposure. The Major was a Union officer and is believed to be her protector. According to the psychics, the Major died thirty or forty years after Emily, and they developed some kind of relationship in the spirit world. It has been suggested that the Major had a little girl of his own and that Emily became his surrogate daughter. A member of the museum staff recently encountered the Major and greeted him with a cheerful, "Hi, Sarge!" The spirit turned and angrily stalked away, apparently offended at being addressed as someone of inferior rank.

One psychic who visited Hupp's Hill claims that it is not haunted by one or two or even two hundred ghosts, but by *thousands*. She described crowds of phantoms marching up the road and gathering on the hill in a spectral mob; it's apparently so crowded they're even up in the trees. The psychic couldn't say what the specters were doing there, but one possible explanation can be found in ancient mythology. Many cultures, including the Greeks and Mayans, believed that spirits had to travel through certain caves to reach the underworld. Perhaps Crystal Caverns is one of those places and Hupp's Hill is a kind of waiting room for the dead.

3.

GHOSTS
OF THE EARTH

From underground caves to above-ground volcanoes, the United States is filled with spectacular land formations. But such places have a long, not always happy, history. Is it any wonder, then, that they should also have their own set of spirits, from ghosts haunting a cave to a pair of mysterious pants?

MAMMOTH CAVE

The wooded hills of central Kentucky sit on top of hundreds of miles of natural corridors that make up Mammoth Cave, one of the biggest caves on Earth and the scene of more than 150 ghostly encounters. No doubt many of these were tricks of light or the result of strange cave acoustics, but it's experienced guides, not tourists, who report the most dramatic experiences. Invisible hands have shoved them in the dark; they've seen figures dressed in nineteenth-century clothing, heard unexplained voices, and had their candles and torches mysteriously blown out. Much of this activity is blamed on three ghosts: the spirits of Stephen Bishop, "Melissa," and Floyd Collins.

In the nineteenth century, Mammoth Cave belonged to a man named Franklin Gorin, who opened it to visitors and had his slaves conduct tours. Among them was Stephen Bishop, who went on to explore the cave and name many of its features. He found blindfish in the river and the bones of an extinct cave bear, drew maps, and, what was remarkable for the time, received full credit for his work. Bishop died in 1857 and was buried above the cave where he spent his life—and is apparently spending his death. Guides describe a figure in a Panama hat who joins their group, says nothing, and vanishes before the tour ends. Attempts to find the missing man are always unsuccessful, but he is believed by many to be Bishop, who always wore a broad-brimmed hat and apparently pops in from time to time to revisit the place he loved.

The second specter, "Melissa," is more mysterious. She was first mentioned in a magazine article from 1858, which told the story of a girl named Melissa, who grew up near Mammoth Cave and fell in love with her tutor, Mr. Beverleigh from Boston. Mr. Beverleigh did not return her affections, and when he began courting another woman, Melissa took revenge. She took him on a tour of the cave and then deliberately abandoned Beverleigh at an underground stream called Echo River. It was meant to be a cruel joke, but he never found his way out, and Melissa, horrified by what she'd done, returned to the cave every day to search for him. Finally, her health gave out, and she died of tuberculosis. There's no proof that Melissa existed, yet a ghost has often been seen in the passageways calling for Beverleigh, and once, when the cave was closed to the public, a witness at Echo River heard coughing, the most recognizable symptom of tuberculosis.

For a brief time, the third ghost was the most famous man in America. Floyd Collins was a cave explorer who discovered Crystal Cave (not to be confused with Crystal Caverns in Virginia), which he operated as a tourist attraction. With Mammoth and other caverns so nearby, competition was fierce. Collins was always looking for new attractions to draw tourists to his cave, although he probably never expected to *be* one.

Left: Stephen Bishop's spirit may still be visiting the caves he spent his life exploring. (COURTESY LIBRARY OF CONGRESS)

WITH MAMMOTH AND OTHER CAVERNS SO NEARBY, COMPETITION WAS FIERCE. COLLINS WAS ALWAYS LOOKING FOR NEW ATTRACTIONS TO DRAW TOURISTS TO HIS CAVE, ALTHOUGH HE PROBABLY NEVER EXPECTED TO *BE* ONE.

In January 1925, Collins was exploring a crumbling passage in Sand Cave when a falling stone left him trapped deep underground. The story became a media sensation, especially after a journalist crawled down the hole and interviewed the trapped man. Tremendous efforts were made to free Collins, but the cave finally collapsed, and he died from exposure and starvation. His story, however, was far from over.

It took months of digging to find the remains and give them a proper burial. In the meantime, Crystal Cave was sold, and, as part of the deal, the new owners were given the right to exhibit the single most famous thing about it—Floyd Collins himself. His body was exhumed, placed in a glass-topped coffin, and put on display even though cave crickets had eaten Collins's ears and part of his face. Collins proved to be a draw, and Crystal Cave became so successful that employees of a rival cave stole him in 1929. When the body was finally returned, a leg was missing. Its whereabouts remains unknown. In 1989, sixty-four years after Floyd Collins died, he was buried for the third and final time, but he is not resting in peace.

Collins's ghost has been accused of dropping bottles on people in Crystal Cave, and members of the staff have heard a man's voice screaming over and over again for "Johnnie" to help him. This is believed to be Floyd's ghost calling for his friend, Johnnie Gerald, the last person to speak with him before the final fatal cave-in. His spirit might also be out searching for that lost leg.

Of course, not every spirit in Mammoth is as serious as Bishop, "Melissa," and Collins. A pair of ghostly pants has also been seen running through the cave by themselves.

Above: Family and friends gather at funeral services for Floyd Collins, whose body was found buried in Sand Cave two weeks after a cave-in left him imprisoned in the debris. (© BETTMANN/CORBIS)

Right: In this 1925 print, a woman ventures too close to the edge of the Grand Canyon. (© B.L. SINGLEY, COURTESY LIBRARY OF CONGRESS)

Keystone View Company,
Manufacturers and Publishers.

GRAND CANYON, HUMBLE GHOST

The Grand Canyon is nature at its most spectacular: soaring stone towers, dizzying cliffs, and the roaring river that carved them. Such a dramatic setting would be expected have an equally impressive ghost, maybe something headless or fiery, yet the canyon is haunted by a very plain specter. It is believed to be the ghost of a woman whose husband and son were killed in a hiking accident sometime in the 1920s. Not long after their deaths, she fell from the north rim of the canyon and has been returning to it ever since.

The "Wandering Woman" appears on the steep North Kaibab Trail. Her head is wrapped in a scarf, and she's wearing a white robe decorated with a pattern of small flowers as she searches for her lost family. When not on the trail, a nearby lodge is haunted by this housewifely apparition.

4.

JUSTICE IS SERVED

Crime in all its forms is a constant feature of ghost stories. Violence, deception, and theft can unsettle the spirits of victims as well as those who commit the crimes. Prisons, which contain whole populations of criminals and where death takes many forms, some of them gruesome, are among the most haunted places in America, but one of them stands alone: literally.

ROCK OF CAGES

San Francisco Bay has always been haunted.

In the 1800s, the clipper ship SS *Tennessee* sank in a heavy fog, and the entire crew was lost. Since then, the ship has returned many times, rolling in with the mist and peacefully sailing beneath the orange span of the Golden Gate Bridge. This bridge has a sinister reputation of its own, but the most evil part of the bay is a bleak outcropping of sandstone where Native Americans believed demons dwelt. This island, which the Spaniards named *Isla de los Alcatraces*, or Island of the Pelicans, after its most obvious residents, was later simplified to "Alcatraz."

At one time, Alcatraz was the most notorious prison in America. Today it's a nature preserve and tourist attraction. But when darkness falls and the ghosts come out, a name given to it by the inmates seems more accurate: "Hellcatraz."

In 1853, the U.S. government began to fortify the island to protect San Francisco from invasion. Alcatraz's remote location, plus the fast currents and frigid water of the bay, made it nearly escape-proof. Then, in 1861, the fortress became a military prison. Soldiers who committed crimes were sent there, along with Confederate prisoners-of-war and, later, Native Americans who resisted government policies. The military jail closed in 1934, around the same time that the Bureau of Prisons decided to put the country's worst criminals under one roof in a place far from the outside world. Alaska was considered, but ultimately they chose Alcatraz.

The buildings were renovated with electricity in the cells, iron bars that could not be broken with tools such as saws and files, and up-to-date security measures. (For example, tear-gas bombs were installed in the ceiling of the cafeteria and could be dropped by pulling a lever.) Daily life was harsh in the new super-prison; inmates could not talk, whistle, or even hum, and punishments were terrible.

The worst was imprisonment in "the Hole," a cold, pitch-black, concrete cell that contained nothing but a straw mat, which was removed during the day. Prisoners were stripped, and then put into the Hole and fed nothing but bread and water. When their punishment was over, many were taken directly to the infirmary. For some, the experience was so traumatic that they went mad.

Alcatraz never held more than 300 inmates at one time, but those it did house were exceptionally dangerous men. There were bank robbers and kidnappers like Alvin "Creepy" Karpis and "Machine-Gun" Kelly, Chicago crime boss "Scarface" Al Capone (who spent his time mopping floors, doing laundry, and playing a banjo), and Robert Stroud, the "Birdman of Alcatraz," a killer who studied birds and their diseases before his transfer to Alcatraz. Stroud's research was forbidden at Alcatraz, where reforming inmates was not on the agenda.

The island of Alcatraz and its famous prison stand alone in San Francisco Bay.
(© BETTMANN/CORBIS)

By the 1960s, the practice of housing inmates without trying to reform them was considered out-of-date, and the cost of operating the prison for so few inmates too high, so Alcatraz closed. The buildings remained, but they were empty except for the retired guards and former prisoners taking visitors on tours. And the ghosts, of course.

Inmates' cells line the walls of Alcatraz. Although they have been empty since the prison closed in 1962, strange sounds can still be heard from time to time.
(COURTESY NATIONAL PARK SERVICE, MUSEUM MANAGEMENT PROGRAM & ALCATRAZ ISLAND, BROADWAY, WWW.CR.NPS.GOV/MUSEUM)

NIGHT WATCHMEN AND GUIDES HAVE HEARD SCREAMS, METALLIC CLANGING NOISES, AND CONVERSATIONS DRIFTING OUT OF EMPTY CELLS AND HALLWAYS.

Vicious criminals, grinding unhappiness, and occasional violence have all left their mark on a place that already had a reputation for demons. Some cells are unnaturally cold, and the long-deserted laundry occasionally fills with the smell of smoke. Night watchmen and guides have heard screams, metallic clanging noises, and conversations drifting out of empty cells and hallways. There's also the sound of running feet and banjo music. Phantom gunfire has been reported, which might be echoes from an unsuccessful escape attempt in 1946 called the "Battle of Alcatraz" that left five dead and eleven injured. Another disturbing phenomenon is the sound of sobbing coming from inside the walls themselves, like a heartbeat inside a chest. It's as though the buildings absorbed a portion of the misery they contained.

Apparitions have also been reported all over the island. Among them are spectral inmates and soldiers from its days as a fortress. But the worst phantom on Alcatraz was "the Thing."

Little is known about the Thing other than claims that it haunted cells 12D and 14D in the isolation block, had glowing red eyes, and killed a prisoner sometime in the 1940s. According to the story, an inmate in one of the solitary confinement cells began screaming that something was in his cell with him. The guards paid no attention, and in the morning the man was found dead with a purple face, bulging eyes, and the mark of a strangler's hands on his throat.

Perhaps the story is nothing more than prison folklore. Maybe it's a supernatural version of a real murder, or even a boogeyman invented to scare new prisoners. These are both reasonable possibilities in the daylight. After sundown, though, when the wind is whistling through the tiers of rusting human cages, it's easy to believe that something red-eyed and murderous wanders the crumbling halls of Hellcatraz.

MORE SPIRITS & CELL BLOCKS

Alcatraz is not the only prison where inmates seem to be serving an eternal sentence. At Pennsylvania's Eastern State Penitentiary, every inmate was kept in solitary confinement and forbidden to speak. This was intended to keep the prisoners away from the poor influence of other convicts, allowing them to think about their mistakes. Guards enforced the silence with the use of straitjackets, metal gags that cut the tongue, and other tortures. Although done with the best intentions, these rules had the unfortunate side effect of driving many prisoners mad.

Eastern State operated from 1829 to 1913 and is now open to the public. Guides, volunteers, and tourists have reported a variety of phenomena: unexplained screams, laughter, and footsteps have been heard in the cells and corridors, although interestingly, the guards wore socks over their boots and walked in silence. Shadows are seen gliding down the halls, a dark figure rushes away when approached, and a phantom guard appears above the walls in the guard tower.

Compared with the ominous bulk of Eastern State, the Burlington County Prison in Mt. Holly, New Jersey, seems small and almost quaint. It served as a prison from 1811 to 1965. During that time, several murders took place in the course of escape attempts. The building held prisoners condemned to death, some of whom were kept chained to the floor in a cell with no fireplace. (The iron ring in the floor is still there.) The dungeon is believed to be haunted by Joel Clough, a young man hanged in the 1830s for fatally stabbing a woman. He has been heard groaning, and ghost hunters have reported electromagnetic phenomena in the cell that they associate with spirits. Joel's body is believed to be somewhere in the prison yard. When an attempt was made to record EVPs on the site of his presumed grave, the tape recorder malfunctioned.

A SPIRITED DEFENSE

Ghosts or poltergeists are seldom mentioned in a court of law, but there are exceptions, and they tend to involve the things that might interest a dead person, such as distributing property or identifying a killer.

On January 23, 1897, a neighbor found the body of twenty-four-year-old Zona Heaster Shue in her home near Livesay's Mill in Greenbrier County, West Virginia. When the doctor arrived, her husband, a blacksmith named Edward S. Shue, was cradling Zona's head in his arms, hysterical with grief; they had been married only three months, and he would not let her go. The doctor was unable to do a proper examination, so he declared her death the result of heart failure and she was buried.

Zona's mother, Mary Heaster, did not accept the doctor's verdict. She had never trusted her son-in-law, who was a stranger to the area, and prayed that her daughter would appear and reveal what really happened. Mary got her wish a few days after the funeral, claiming that Zona's ghost visited her on four consecutive nights and provided a detailed account of her death.

The spirit said that she had prepared a dinner for Edward that he didn't like. He flew into a rage, grabbed her with his powerful blacksmith's hands, and broke her neck. Zona's ghost provided a detailed description of the house and surrounding neighborhood, neither of which her mother had ever seen.

Mary told her friends and neighbors what the ghost had said. Some laughed, but others remembered the way Shue kept people away from the coffin during the wake and used a pillow, a folded sheet, and a scarf to steady Zona's head. At last, Mary

Heaster was able to convince the local prosecuting attorney to take a closer look at her daughter's death.

It turned out that Shue had a prison record and Zona was his *third* wife. One, or possibly both, of the previous Mrs. Shues had died under suspicious circumstances, and the blacksmith had once predicted he would marry seven times.

Zona's body was exhumed and an examination revealed that she had a crushed windpipe and broken neck. Shue was placed on trial, and Mrs. Heaster was questioned about the ghost. Ultimately, Shue was found guilty. He was sentenced to life in prison and died there in 1900.

It was a broken neck, not a ghost, that convicted Edward Shue, but Zona's spirit and her mother's willingness to discuss the experience were instrumental in reopening the case and, possibly, saving the lives of four other women.

FAMOUS PHANTOMS
5. OF FILM LAND

An old movie is like a classic haunting: images of long-dead people flicker into view, go through the same motions over and over again, and then vanish. The line between the two is thin, which might explain why Hollywood, the entertainment capital of the world, produces as many ghosts as it does films. What's more, all the elements of a good haunting are present in movieland: money, mansions, and crowds of people who want to be noticed.

"LIGHTS, CAMERA, . . . HAUNTING!"

Europe has countless stories about passionate kings and queens with tragic lives who became ghosts (Mary Queen of Scots is one of the busiest specters in the United Kingdom), and the same thing happens in Hollywood.

Rudolph Valentino became famous for playing the romantic lead in silent films like *The Sheik* (1921). Valentino lived a flamboyant life and inspired nearly hysterical devotion among his fans, but his marriages failed, and he died at the age of thirty-one.

His death was caused by peritonitis—a fatal inflammation of the abdomen—but there were rumors that a jilted girlfriend or angry husband had murdered him. An estimated 100,000 people attended his funeral in New York City and nearly rioted. The windows of the funeral parlor were smashed, and an endless line of mourners stood waiting for a glimpse of the star in his casket. (According to legend, a wax model of Valentino was used instead of the real body. He looked terrible after a long, painful death, and ghoulish fans kept trying to snip bits of his hair and clothing as souvenirs.) A second enormous funeral was held in Los Angeles, and the man known as "the Great Lover" was finally buried in Hollywood. It was a short, eventful life, and his ghost maintains a full schedule of haunting.

Rudolph Valentino, "the Great Lover," seems to be even more active in death than he was in life. His ghost has been seen throughout California. (COURTESY LIBRARY OF CONGRESS)

Valentino appears in the bedroom and hallways of Falcon's Lair, his Beverly Hills mansion, as well as in the stable where he kept his horses. The actor's spirit is also believed to pace the porch of his former beach house near Oxnard. A figure dressed in Valentino's desert costume has been seen walking on a nearby beach without leaving footprints in the sand. Valentino appears at other locations in California as well, including the Santa Maria Inn, in Santa Maria, California; Valentino Place, an apartment building in Hollywood; and the costume department at Paramount Studios. A lady in black has also been seen outside Valentino's crypt in the Hollywood Memorial Park in Hollywood. Strangely, he has not appeared in New York City, where he died. Maybe it's the weather.

A HAUNTED MIRROR

Marilyn Monroe was one of the most famous stars to ever come out of Hollywood, but she did not have a happy life and was only thirty-six years old when she died (under suspicious circumstances) in 1962. Monroe often stayed in Suite 1200 of the Hollywood Roosevelt Hotel in a room that contained a full-length mirror. Naturally she was often reflected in it, and even though the actress is long gone, her image lingers in the glass. The mirror now hangs in a hallway of the Hollywood Roosevelt, offering guests a chance to do some celebrity ghost watching while waiting for the elevator. Monroe's ghost is also supposed to appear by her grave in Westwood Memorial Park and at the house in Brentwood where she died.

THELMA TODD'S FATE REMAINS A CLASSIC HOLLYWOOD MYSTERY WITH A SUPERNATURAL FOOTNOTE.

A MYSTERIOUS PHONE CALL

Hollywood and Beverly Hills are dotted with mansions where the stars of yesteryear still go bump in the night. Jean Harlow, Buster Keaton, Mary Pickford, and Clifton Webb are all supposed to haunt their former homes with unexplained noises, object movement, and an occasional apparition. George Reeves's ghost has even been seen wearing his Superman costume. But a more unusual phenomenon occurred after the death of Thelma Todd.

Todd planned to be a schoolteacher, but instead she went to California and became a movie star. She was in dozens of movies and shorts, appeared with the Marx Brothers and Laurel and Hardy, and even opened a successful restaurant. Then on the morning of December 16, 1935, the actress was found dead. She was decked out in jewels, wore a silver gown and mink coat, and was slumped over the wheel of her car. The garage door was closed and the engine running, still pumping out the carbon monoxide that killed her.

Police were baffled; she wasn't upset or depressed, and the drops of blood in Todd's nose raised the possibility of violence. An investigation was carried out, but the more the police learned, the more confusing everything became. Witnesses made contradictory statements and seemed to be covering up *something*, though to this day no one knows what. Her death was finally ruled an accident with an unwritten question mark next to it. Thelma Todd's fate remains a classic Hollywood mystery with a supernatural footnote.

During the investigation, Mrs. Wallace Ford testified that she had received a phone call from Todd on Sunday afternoon at around four-thirty. The actress had been invited to a party at Ford's house and wanted to know if she could bring a guest; Todd playfully refused to say who the guest was, but promised Ford that she would be surprised.

Mrs. Ford *was* surprised, especially when she learned that this conversation had taken place eleven to twelve hours *after* her friend had died. Todd's ghost has since been seen repeatedly by park rangers and hikers near her home.

Left: Thelma Todd, shown here, is said to have placed one last phone call, some eleven or twelve hours after her death. (© BETTMANN/CORBIS)
Right: California's instantly recognizable HOLLYWOOD sign once read "HOLLYWOODLAND"—an advertisement for a nearby real estate development. (© BETTMANN/CORBIS)

HOLLYWOODLAND

It should come as no surprise that the symbol of Hollywood itself is haunted.

In 1923, an enormous sign with letters thirty feet wide and fifty feet high was built on Mt. Lee to advertise a real estate development called HOLLYWOODLAND. The "land" part was removed a few years later, but "HOLLYWOOD" remained as a permanent landmark. Then the ghost came along.

Park rangers have had numerous encounters with the phantom of a beautiful woman dressed in 1930s-style clothing. Leashed dogs pull to get away from her, but the figure soon evaporates, leaving a flowery scent behind.

She is believed to be Peg Entwistle, a twenty-four-year-old British actress who was killed in a fall from the letter "H" in 1932. Electronic sensors installed to protect the sign from vandals often detect a presence when no one visible is there, and the strong sweet smell of Peg's trademark gardenia perfume is reported year round.

Although she appeared in only one film, Peg Entwistle's unique combination of ghosts and gardenias has made her an enduring part of Hollywood mythology.

SILVER SCREAMS

The old saying "Every good theater has a ghost" refers to traditional theaters with stages, dressing rooms, and scenery. But does this mean the local multiplex can't be haunted? Not at all. In fact, spooks seem to thrive in an atmosphere of make-believe, whether it smells of greasepaint or popcorn.

Movie palaces—like other palaces—are often haunted. Hollywood's famed Pantages Theater has several ghosts, including a tall apparition believed to be the spirit of its former owner, Howard Hughes. Hughes was an eccentric billionaire who wore tissue boxes for slippers and is believed to have been seen visiting his old office. And at the Tampa Theater in Florida, the mischievous spirit of a former projectionist not only opens and closes doors but also steals small objects and taps people on the shoulder as well. These grand movie houses can't compare with the Skowhegan Strand Cinema in Skowhegan, Maine, however, when it comes to being haunted.

Built in 1929, the theater and a small apartment attached to it have reputedly been the scene of various unpleasant phenomena. Tools have been thrown, and workmen suffered electrical shocks despite the power being turned off. When a former owner tried redecorating, she placed an open can of paint on a stepladder, stepped out of the room for a moment, and returned to find the can undisturbed but the walls dripping with spattered paint. There are stories about cold spots, and a shadowy figure in the balcony once threw a piece of the ceiling onto the seats below. Mysterious handprints are also supposed to appear on the movie screen, and a young patron recently complained about phantom fingers poking her head and back while she watched a film.

Chicago's Biograph Theater is also haunted, but its famous ghost appears outside the building. On the night of July 22, 1934, a gangster movie called *Manhattan Melodrama* was playing at the theater. When the film ended, the audience exited onto Lincoln Avenue. Shots were fired, and a man in a straw hat pulled out a gun, ran down an alley, and fell down dead. Public Enemy Number One, John Dillinger, had been ambushed and shot dead by FBI agents—probably.

There have always been doubts about who was really gunned down that night. Dillinger's appearance had been altered through plastic surgery, and a small-time criminal who resembled him allegedly disappeared around the same time. Rumors claim that the look-alike was killed while the real Dillinger went into hiding and died many years later. It seems unlikely, however, that someone who loved robbing banks as much as John Dillinger could simply give it up.

Lingering doubts about what happened might be reflected in the haunting itself, which takes the form of a blurry figure that runs down the alley, collapses, and disappears. Is it Dillinger? We'll never know, but violence and sudden death seem to have left a permanent supernatural mark on the Biograph.

This sign, displaying Public Enemy Number One, John Dillinger, hung in police stations across the nation until his supposed death in July 1934. (© BETTMANN/CORBIS)

6.

Life in the Old West was not just shoot-outs, Indian raids, and stampedes. Most people, whether settlers or Native Americans, spent their time doing the hard work needed to survive in a harsh land. Violence was a daily feature of life, however, and it left its supernatural footprint, or "bootprint," in many places, including a town with a name that's synonymous with death.

GHOST TOWN

The town of Tombstone, Arizona, was a much livelier place than the name suggests. It is a town full of ghosts, although it is by no means a ghost town. The term "ghost town" is used to describe the hastily constructed settlements created when a gold strike or other opportunity attracted thousands of men to the middle of nowhere. When the gold gave out, the makeshift town was abandoned as quickly as it went up. This should have been Tombstone's fate when the silver mines closed, but it was the administrative center of Cochise County and managed to survive. At its height, the city had 15,000 residents. Its central attraction was the Bird Cage Opera House Saloon, which was described by *The New York Times* as "the wildest, roughest, wickedest honky-tonk between Basin Street and the Barbary

TODAY, THE BUILDING IS A MUSEUM WITH EXHIBITS THAT INCLUDE DOC HOLLIDAY'S GAMBLING TABLE, PLAYING CARDS, PHOTOGRAPHS, AND THE CITY HEARSE (CALLED THE "BLACK MARIA"); THERE'S ALSO A LESS CONVENTIONAL COLLECTION OF PHANTOM TOMBSTONERS STILL ENJOYING THEMSELVES AT THE BIRD CAGE.

Coast." The Bird Cage provided the residents of Tombstone with the expensive, unwholesome entertainment they craved.

With its long, narrow shape having been compared to a coffin, the building was one of the solidest structures in town—it needed to be to survive the constant fighting—and was made of stone when almost everything else was shabbily constructed out of wood. Visitors walked through the double doors into a cloud of cigar smoke and the roar of laughter, shouting, and music. The floor was crowded with miners and gamblers. Overhead, two rows of balconies ran along opposite sides of the room; these were the "birdcages," private boxes with red drapes where beautiful ladies poured champagne and entertained friends. Games of chance and refreshments of every sort were available, and the grand piano played while a woman stood on the stage warbling a tune. Her song was sometimes interrupted by gunfire, but it didn't take long to drag out the remains and get back to being wicked; after all, the Bird Cage had a reputation to uphold.

For nine years, the doors were always open. Men like Doc Holliday, Wyatt Earp, and the Clanton brothers spent much of their time and money there. In the theater's brief but lively existence, there were sixteen gun and knife fights and enough shootings to leave nearly 150 bullets embedded in the walls, floor, and ceiling. In the basement, a high-stakes poker game went on without a break for almost eight and half years, during which time ten million dollars changed hands. Today, the building is a museum with exhibits that include Doc Holliday's gambling table, playing cards, photographs, and the city hearse (called the "Black Maria"); there's also a less conventional collection of phantom Tombstoners still enjoying themselves at the Bird Cage.

Witnesses report the sounds of laughter and piano music coming from empty rooms, as well as the smells of cigar smoke and strong perfume. Objects are moved, including electrical cords, heavy card tables, and the hat on the mannequin of Wyatt Earp, which kept getting knocked off when it was exhibited in the Clanton brothers' favorite spot. (Earp shot them during a gunfight at the O.K. Corral, and it's possible that they still bear a grudge.) Apparitions are seen wearing nineteenth-century clothes, including the theater's most persistent ghost, a man with a visor and striped pants who walks across the stage carrying a clipboard.

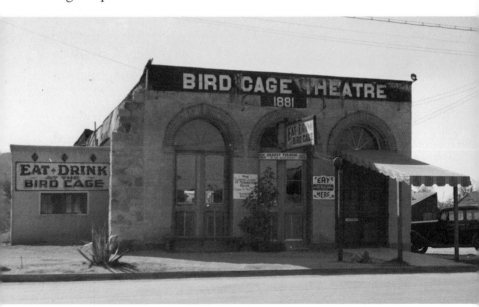

The Bird Cage Theatre (also known as "The Bird Cage Opera House Saloon"), in Tombstone, Arizona, was known as "the wildest, roughest, wickedest honky-tonk between Basin Street and the Barbary Coast." (COURTESY LIBRARY OF CONGRESS)

One of the bloodiest episodes in the saloon's history also left its mark. A woman called "Gold Dollar" was involved with the gambler Billy Milgreen. When a beautiful girl named Margarita sat down in Milgreen's lap, Gold Dollar was understandably annoyed. She cut out Margarita's heart with a knife and left town. The knife is now on display in the museum. The violence of that act still affects sensitive people; in one case, Gold Dollar's ghost is said to have repeatedly stabbed a psychic who was trying to enter the Bird Cage, causing shortness of breath and pressure on her chest.

But Tombstone's spirits aren't all connected to the saloon. A woman in a white dress haunts the street near the courthouse, and a man in a frock coat crosses the road by the old Wells Fargo building and then disappears. A ride on the Black Maria would lead you to Boot Hill, the site of a particularly interesting manifestation.

Terry "Ike" Clanton (a descendant of the Clanton brothers) was at the cemetery one day taking photographs of a friend dressed in cowboy gear. The friend posed with the headstones behind him and the Dragoon Mountains in the distance, while Clanton took black-and-white pictures for an old-fashioned look. When the film came back, however, one photograph contained more than the Old West atmosphere.

In the middle ground, among the desert plants and grave markers, is a figure that seems half-buried in the ground. It looks male and thin, seems to be dressed in shirtsleeves, and has a broad-brimmed black hat on its head. (Some people think that the figure is holding a knife, but it's hard to see in reproductions.) Clanton denies any trickery, and it's hard to explain the image as a chance combination of light and shadows. Boot Hill itself looks strange in the picture as well. It's overgrown and neglected, the way it might have looked before proper maintenance began in the 1940s. On the face of it, the picture seems to be of a ghost half-risen out of the earth, although why the cemetery should need weeding is anyone's guess.

Tombstonites lying under the sod of Boot Hill might be restless, but they'll never be lonely. Long before the first Conestoga wagon came rolling across the plains, the southwest had a thriving population of Native American and Spanish ghouls: everything from dead Navajo that return in the shape of a whirlwind to spread terror and illness, to La Llorona, the donkey-headed spirit of a woman who murdered her children and spends eternity searching for them. The Wild West, with its cowboys, prospectors, barmaids, and railroad workers, merely added a new element to what has always been one of the most haunted corners of Haunted U.S.A.

ANNABELLE OF ST. ELMO

St. Elmo, Colorado was a classic boomtown. Silver was discovered there in 1878, and from 1880 to the 1920s, it was a thriving town with a population of between one and two thousand.

When the mines closed, the railroads stopped coming and almost everyone left—except the Stark family. The Starks owned the general store and a hotel called the Stark Home Comfort Inn. As others left, they bought up the town's property, believing that the town would eventually be revived. By the time the post office closed and St. Elmo officially vanished in 1952, only the Stark children, Tony and Annabelle, remained.

Little has been written about Tony, but Annabelle was known as the "Queen of St. Elmo" for her beauty, education, and, perhaps, the family's sense of their own importance. As Annabelle grew older, though, she became less regal. She no longer washed, filled the hotel with trash, and patrolled the town with a rifle. The store remained open for its few remaining customers, but the Queen of St. Elmo had become known as "Dirty Annie."

In 1958, Annabelle had an auto accident. Shortly afterward, she was sent to a mental hospital, where she lived until her death in 1960.

Not long after Annabelle's death, there were a series of odd events at the Home Comfort Inn. Children playing in one of the rooms were frightened by the doors all slamming shut and a sudden drop in temperature. As the hotel was being renovated, tools and cleaning supplies that were put away every night were found in the middle of the floor every morning, even after being locked up. The only mention of an apparition was a beautiful young woman in white seen in a second-story bedroom window of the hotel.

A witness saw her from the street, then saw some people in snowmobiles and asked them to leave (snowmobiles aren't allowed in the town). After they left, the mysterious woman nodded down from the window in apparent gratitude.

There's no mention of additional phenomena, but some believe that the Queen of St. Elmo still reigns and that Annabelle Stark watches over the town.

7. TALES FROM THE BONEYARD

Many modern cemeteries don't look like cemeteries at all. Instead of tombstones, identical plaques are screwed flat into the lawn to make mowing and watering easier for the groundskeeper. The results look more like a golf course than a graveyard, and one wonders if ghosts are willing to appear in a place without mossy crypts, lopsided tombstones, or statues of angels pointing at the sky. Despite their reputation, cemeteries don't seem to be particularly haunted. There are exceptions, though, like Bachelor's Grove in Midlothian outside Chicago, a city with strong claims as the Haunted Graveyard Capital of the United States.

BACHELOR'S GROVE

At the end of a gravel path in the Rubio Woods Forest Preserve lies a neglected cemetery where knee-high weeds grow over cracked and broken tombstones. There are many mysteries here, beginning with the name "Bachelor's Grove." No one knows what it means or where it comes from.

The land may have belonged to someone named Bachelor, or it could have been a popular spot for burying unmarried men. What's certain is that the cemetery opened in 1844 and had

TENNESSEE HAS SKINNED TOM, WHO CARRIES A KNIFE AND HAS NO SKIN; THERE'S AN AXE-SWINGING GOATMAN IN MARYLAND; AND OHIO IS HOME TO ORANGE EYES, A GIANT WITH GLOWING ORANGE EYES. A TWO-HEADED GHOST THAT RISES FROM A CEMETERY POND WOULD FIT RIGHT IN.

fallen into disuse by the late 1980s. Its isolation and general creepiness made it an attractive lover's lane, and there were rumors about Satanists conducting rituals there. Grave markers were spray-painted, broken, and stolen (which might explain the legend about tombstones changing their locations from time to time). Many of the stones are believed to be at the bottom of the algae-choked pond that plays a part in many Bachelor's Grove legends; it's a small body of water with a sinister reputation.

In the nineteenth century, a farmer was plowing his field when his horse fell into the pond, pulling the man in with it: both drowned. And during Prohibition, Chicago's battling gangsters found the pond a convenient place to leave bodies they didn't need anymore. Both of these events seem to have left a supernatural residue.

The ghosts of the farmer and his horse have been seen plowing in Bachelor's Grove, while visitors driving away from the cemetery have been hit by a vintage black automobile. There's a tremendous grinding crash, parts go flying through the air, and then the strange car vanishes. Drivers are shaken but unhurt, and their vehicles are left without a scratch. No one knows where the black car came from, though it might be reenacting a trip to the cemetery's informal floating morgue. But the oddest apparition connected to the pool is a genuine rarity: a two-headed ghost.

Little is known about this particular phantom, but it might date from Bachelor's Grove's days as a lover's lane, because there's something about kissing couples that attracts unusual spooks. Tennessee has Skinned Tom, who carries a knife and has no skin; there's an axe-swinging Goatman in Maryland; and Ohio is home to Orange Eyes, a giant with glowing orange eyes. A two-headed ghost that rises from a cemetery pond would fit right in.

Bachelor's Grove has other, more standard phenomena as well, like strange sounds and blue lights flitting through the woods. But it's best-known for its apparitions; one of them even posed for a picture.

On August 10, 1991, ghost-hunter Jude Huff-Felz's camera captured a remarkable image in Bachelor's Grove. Instead of the usual blurs and mists, the high-speed infrared film showed a woman dressed in a long gown seated, with ankles primly crossed, on a tombstone. She is believed to be the "White Lady," or "Madonna of Bachelor's Grove," a ghost in a white dress seen walking through the cemetery carrying a baby. In addition to the woman in white, the cemetery also has a glowing Yellow Man, but little is known about him.

Another puzzling apparition is a white farmhouse with pillars in front, a porch swing, and lights burning in the windows. It is seen on the path leading to the cemetery and vanishes when approached. No building resembling the house ever stood in that area, and no firsthand eyewitness accounts exist, yet the story is widely told. Perhaps people are seeing a very rare sort of apparition, the ghost of a house that hasn't been built yet.

SPOOK HOUSES

What's more haunted than a house with ghosts? A house that *is* a ghost. The wandering farmhouse that appears outside Bachelor's Grove Cemetery is unusual, but not unique. A woman in Mincy, Missouri, for example, saw a cabin with smoke curling out of its chimney that was gone the next day. The neighbors knew nothing about it and said that, as far as they knew, no cabin had ever stood on that spot.

A home that did exist was the Cosgrove Mansion of Northport, Maine. On December 16, 1954, it caught fire and burned to the ground, leaving five people dead. The site remains empty apart from some pieces of the foundation and a chimney that stands by itself in the vacant lot. According to legend, the mansion can still be seen, but instead of shimmering into view on the anniversary of its destruction like most ghosts, it only appears on film. Taking photographs of the spot where the Cosgrove Mansion stood is said to produce images of the house looking the way it did before the accident.

CEMETERY STATUES

Bachelor's Grove isn't Chicago's only haunted cemetery. The spirit of a weeping woman haunts Archer Woods Cemetery, and phantom monks float through St. James at Sag Bridge Churchyard. Graceland Cemetery is home to several ghosts, along with something even more unusual.

The tomb of six-year-old Inez Clarke is decorated with the fine marble statue of a little girl, enclosed in a clear protective box. On rainy nights, though, when there's lightning and thunder, the statue crawls out of the box, climbs down from its pedestal, and goes walking around Graceland.

Left: The marble statue atop Inez Clarke's grave may seem innocent by day, but on rainy nights she has been said to climb out of her box and go for a walk around the cemetery. (© RICHIE DIESTERHEFT)

Right: The tombstone of Felix Agnus, which once housed the original Black Aggie statue, now sits empty. (© ADRIAN MONACO)

Statues that sit still (or seem to) are sometimes more danger-ous that those that move. Many seated female figures with out-stretched arms have nicknames like "Black Aggie" or "Black Agnes" and are said to kill. Legends about killer statues can be found all over the country, but the original Black Aggie decorated the grave of Felix Agnus, a Union general during the Civil War. (The name "Aggie" apparently comes from "Agnus.") He is buried in Druid Ridge Cemetery in Baltimore, Maryland, where Black Aggie became part of local sorority and fraternity initiations. In most stories, a girl trying to join a sorority had to spend the night sitting in Aggie's lap. The next morning, her body was found on the statue, covered with marks that suggest she died in the clutches of a superhuman grip. The "Witch's Chair" in St. James Episcopal Cemetery in Bristol, Pennsylvania, has a legend similar to Black Aggie's. Those sitting in the wrought-iron chair at midnight in October will find themselves wrapped in the arms of a ghostly witch. There are also reports of a female apparition being sighted in the chair.

Perhaps it's best not to look too closely at these statues. Aggie's eyes are said to give off a burning glare at midnight that blinds anyone foolish enough to stare into them. And gazing at the eyes of "Eternal Silence," a tall, robed figure in Chicago's Graceland Cemetery, has a more unusual effect; it gives people visions of their own death.

TOMBS THAT MADE THEIR MARK

It's widely believed that a person's spirit lingers by his or her grave. As a result, one particular crypt in New Orleans' St. Louis Cemetery No. 1 has become a popular destination for people seeking supernatural help.

A plaque fastened to the outside reads:

Marie Laveau
This Greek Revival tomb is reputed burial place of this notorious
"Voodoo Queen." A mystic cult, Voodooism, of African origin, was brought
to this city from Santo Domingo and flourished in 19th century. Marie
Laveau was the most widely known of many practitioners of the cult.

Laveau's (1801?–1881?) reputation as a sorceress survives to this day. According to rumor, so does Laveau herself, which would make the voodoo priestess one of the most buried people alive. At least three graves in New Orleans are believed to be her final resting place. People who ask her spirit for help leave gifts of coins and flowers and draw an X on the wall of the tomb. (The crypt in St. Louis Cemetery No. 1 is covered with Xs.)

Laveau's tomb is not the only crypt with unusual marks. The ornate marble mausoleum of the Craigmiles family in Cleveland, Tennessee, was built in the churchyard of St. Luke's Episcopal Church and first used for seven-year-old Nina Craigmiles (1864–1871), who died in a collision with a train. Since then, so many Craigmiles have died sudden, premature deaths that bloody marks appeared on the white stonework of the crypt. These stains grew darker every time another member of the family was entombed, and neither cleaning nor replacing certain stones has removed them.

Nina's spirit is also said to haunt the mausoleum, attacking anyone who walks around it thirteen times and then knocks on the door.

The tomb of Marie Laveau in St. Louis Cemetery No. 1 has been covered in Xs by visitors seeking help from Laveau's spirit. (© ROBERT HOLMES/CORBIS)

8. GHOSTS AFLOAT

The ocean is a dangerous place where storms, hidden reefs, and accidents lie in wait for unsuspecting sailors. Those who survive Mother Nature and Lady Luck must also contend with pirates at sea and on the land. ("Land pirates" or "wreckers" used to light fires on rocky coasts to attract ships and cause them to crash. They would then take the cargo that washed ashore.) American ships have been sailing for hundreds of years, and with so many ways to die, there's no shortage of nautical ghosts.

FORECAST: FAIR TO SPOOKY

In January 1647, a top-heavy ship sailed for England from New Haven, Connecticut, carrying valuable goods and several important Puritans. Nothing was heard about it for several months, and it was feared the "Great Shippe" was lost.

One day, some six months later, a violent thunderstorm hammered New Haven. The sky cleared, and the lost vessel came sailing into the harbor! People came out to meet it, but the ship—and only the ship—seemed to be in the grip of a gale. It rocked violently, the masts snapped, and the ship fell over before dissolving into a cloud. Much of New Haven saw the event and believed that it was a reenactment of the real ship's fate.

It is not unusual for ghost ships to be associated with bad weather. They are seen in storms and fog, and many appear to be on fire. According to legend, one of these fiery specters was the result of a terrible crime. In 1738, the crew of the Dutch ship *Palatine* killed their captain, robbed the passengers, and then escaped on boats off the coast of Rhode Island. The vessel washed up on Block Island, where wreckers plundered what was left and set the ship on fire. One passenger became hysterical and refused to leave, so the burning hulk drifted away with her shrieking inside. Since then, a fiery vessel called the "Palatine Light" has been making regular appearances off Block Island, accompanied by the screams of a madwoman.

THE HAUNTED QUEEN

Sometimes a boat's worst enemy is another boat. On March 7, 1866, the fishing schooner *Charles Haskell* of Boston was anchored at George's Bank off the coast of New England with other fishing boats when a vessel got loose and drove the *Haskell* into another craft, the *Andrew Jackson*, which was cut in two. It sank so quickly the entire crew was lost.

The *Haskell* was not badly damaged, but the next time it dropped anchor at George's Bank, it caught more than codfish. Each night, the twenty-six spirits of the *Andrew Jackson*'s crew climbed out of the sea and onto the deck, where they silently went through the motions of steering, fishing, and tending invisible nets on the *Charles Haskell*. After that, no one was willing to work on the ship, and it had to be sold.

Seventy-six years later, during World War II, a similar accident occurred on a much larger scale. An ocean liner nicknamed the

The Queen Mary—now permanently docked in Long Beach, California—served as a troop ship known as the "Grey Ghost" during World War II. Today she is America's most haunted ship. (© Lake County Museum/Corbis)

6A-HI598

"Grey Ghost" was carrying thousands of American troops across the Atlantic when it rammed into the light cruiser HMS *Curacoa*. The *Curacoa* was cut in two. Enemy submarines prevented the Grey Ghost from picking up the survivors, and 338 sailors died. After the war, the grey camouflage paint was stripped off, and the ocean liner went back to being one of the most celebrated ships at sea, the *Queen Mary*.

Built from 1930 to 1934 (with a break during the Great Depression), the finished liner was approximately 1,000 feet long and 180 feet high. She was not the biggest ship afloat, but for many years she was the fastest. During the war, the *Queen Mary*'s size and speed made her an ideal troop ship, and she routinely carried 15,000 soldiers at a time. Hitler's U-boats couldn't sink her, but nature tried to in 1942 when a giant freak wave slammed into the ship and brought her within inches of capsizing. The liner survived the war and the sea, and is permanently moored at Long Beach, California. Visitors can shop, spend the night, attend conventions, and if the stories are true, meet a few of the *Queen Mary*'s eternal residents.

While the ship does not have a distinctly unhappy history, incidents have left their mark. A television crew, for example, made an audiotape of what sounded like the destruction of the *Curacoa*. In addition, about fifty people have died on the liner from various causes. In 1966, an eighteen-year-old crewmember was killed when watertight door number thirteen crushed him in the engine room. Since then, a bearded young man in coveralls has been seen patrolling the area and vanishing next to the fatal door. Most of the other ghosts are harder to explain. It's possible that they were having such a good time, they just decided to stay.

The old first-class lounge (the Queen's Salon), for example, is home to a beautiful phantom in a white evening gown who is often seen dancing alone. Less dramatic but equally odd phenomena are reported in the staterooms. Lights and water faucets turn themselves on, the telephone rings when no one is calling, and something tugs at the sheets at night. The most haunted part of the ship, however, is said to be the swimming pool. Witnesses have reported seeing figures in period swimsuits, and wet footprints appear on the floor leading from the pool (which contains no water) to the changing room.

Sailors are notably superstitious people, so being haunted is not normally good for business. It doomed the *Charles Haskell*, but the *Queen Mary* is retired and happily offers haunted tours (with actors playing the spirits), ghost-hunting expeditions, and lectures by psychics.

PHANTOM ON THE RAILS

America was explored by ship, boat, and canoe, but it was tied together by railroads. Trains made it possible to travel great distances at unheard of speeds. Progress, however, came at a price. Locomotives derailed, collided, exploded, and produced many casualties. With so much blood on the tracks, there are bound to be ghosts, and in many cases, it's the trains themselves that come whistling back from the other side.

On August 27, 1891, a passenger train in North Carolina left Statesville for Asheville. It was halfway across the Bostian Bridge when the locomotive went off the tracks and fell ninety feet; the loss of life was terrible, and those who survived were injured. One year later, on the anniversary of the accident, people heard a tremendous crash and screaming coming from the direction of the bridge. When help arrived, the would-be rescuers found nothing there but a baggage-master who checked his watch and vanished before their eyes. Then in 1941, a woman saw a reenactment of the wreck. To this day, the sound of the train falling off Bostian Bridge is still heard every August 27 at 3 a.m.

President Abraham Lincoln's funeral train is also said to reappear every year, following the route it took from Washington, D.C., to Springfield, Illinois, in 1865. The most dramatic accounts say that two ghostly locomotives are seen with skeletons onboard and funeral music playing. Other reports describe a more conventional phantom train, sounds of train whistles, and puffs of smoke.

CONCLUSION

There are many different ways to think about ghosts.

For some, they're nothing more than errors of perception, what the skeptical Ebenezer Scrooge described as the result of a "slight disorder of the stomach . . . an undigested bit of beef, a blot of mustard, a crumb of cheese, a fragment of an underdone potato." Many see them as a genuine phenomenon involving the soul or spirit, which of course raises questions about the souls and spirits of locomotives, farmhouses, and other inanimate objects that come back as ghosts. Others have little interest in spooks themselves and see them as an expression of people's values and beliefs; for this group, ghosts are a way of learning about the living, not the dead.

There is something about ghost stories, however, that rises above attempts to use or understand them. They entertain us, excite our sense of wonder, and send the same cold shiver down our spines that men and woman have felt since the first tale of spirits and ghouls was told around a crackling fire countless centuries ago. With that in mind, let's have just one more: the tale of a man named Doug.

When Doug was about twenty years old, he was living near Minneapolis and working in a print shop. He went out with friends one night, got back to his apartment sometime after midnight, and flopped down on the sofa to watch TV.

Doug wasn't there long when his neck began prickling; it was the feeling of being watched, and he knew the ghost was back.

He'd seen it two or three times before but had glanced away, and it had disappeared. This time he kept both eyes on the figure and got up for a closer look.

A phantom old lady stood there, though "stood" might not be the right word since her figure disappeared below the knees and hung in the air. She was over five feet tall, looked somewhere between seventy-five and eighty-five years old, and was wearing a typical "grandma" dress, plus a shawl or sweater. Also, the ghost had no color; it was like a three-dimensional black-and-white photograph.

Doug put out his hand to see if she was solid, but his fingers felt like they had gone into frozen air, and then the specter "vaporized."

He didn't mind being haunted. In fact, dirty dishes that he left in the sink were sometimes found mysteriously washed and put away, so twenty-five years later, Doug still enjoys telling the story of "the ghost that did my dishes."

It's something to remember when you're lying in bed at night wondering about that funny noise in the hall; ghosts aren't always gruesome or scary. Sometimes they're just grandmas that don't like a mess.

CHAPTER NOTES

The following notes consist of citations to the sources of quoted material. Each citation includes the first and last words or phrases of the quotation, and its source. References are to works cited in the Selected Bibliography, beginning on page 84. Abbreviations used are:

Interview—Interview conducted by author
King—*Danse Macabre*
WH—WhiteHouse.gov
NYT—*The New York Times*
Dickens—*A Christmas Carol*

Preface
Page
vii   "She had . . . 1800s": Interview
vii   "I could see . . . disappeared": Interview

Introduction
Page
ix   "Unsavory History": King, page 267

Chapter One: America's Most Haunted Houses
Page
4   "I have never . . . remarkable": WH

Chapter Six: That Frontier Spirit
Page
55   "The wildest . . . Barbary Coast": NYT

Conclusion
Page
78   "Slight disorder . . . potato": Dickens, pages 21-22
79   "The ghost . . . dishes": Interview

SOURCES

Adi-Kent, Jeffrey Thomas. *Ghosts in the Valley*. Liberty Twp, OH: Hampton Pub. Co, 1971.

Anson, Jay. *The Amityville Horror*. Englewood Cliffs, NJ: Prentice-Hall, 1977.

Beck, Horace P. *The Folklore of Maine*. Philadelphia: J.B. Lippincott Company, 1957.

Belanger, Jeff. *The World's Most Haunted Places: From the Secret Files of Ghostvillage.com*. Franklin Lakes, NJ: New Page Books, 2004.

Blanche, Tony, and Brad Schreiber. *Death in Paradise*. Los Angeles, CA: General Pub. Group, 1998.

Brunvand, Jan Harold. *The Vanishing Hitchhiker: American Urban Legends and Their Meanings*. New York: W.W. Norton & Company, 1982.

Clyne, Patricia Edwards. *Strange and Supernatural Animals*. New York: Dodd, Mead & Company, 1979.

Dickens, Charles. *A Christmas Carol*. New York: Puffin, 2001.

Guider, Elizabeth. "Showbiz Swooned over Valentino's Demise." *Variety*, September 2005.

Guiley, Rosemary Ellen. *The Encyclopedia of Ghosts and Spirits*. New York: Facts on File, 1992.

Huyghe, Patrick, and Hilary Evans. *The Field Guide to Ghosts and Other Apparitions*. New York; Quill, 2000.

Hauck, Dennis William. *Haunted Places: The National Directory: Ghostly Abodes, Sacred Sites, UFO Landings, and Other Supernatural Locations*. New York: Penguin Books, 2002.

King, Stephen. *Stephen King's Danse Macabre*. New York: Berkley Books, 1981 (2001 printing).

McNeil, W. K., ed. *Ghost Stories from the American South*. Little Rock, AK: August House, 1985.

Norman, Michael, and Beth Scott. *Haunted Heritage: A Definitive Collection of North American Ghost Stories*. New York: Tor Books, 2006.

Rogo, D. Scott. *The Poltergeist Experience*. New York: Penguin Books, 1979.

Weisberg, Barbara. *Talking to the Dead*. San Francisco: Harper One, 2005.

Winer, Richard, and Nancy Osborn. *Haunted Houses*. Toronto/London: Bantam Books, 1979.

WEBSITES

www.alcatrazhistory.com

www.morrisjumel.org

www.nps.gov/gett/ [Gettysburg National Military Park]

www.nps.gov/maca/ [Mammoth Cave National Park]

www.queenmary.com

www.whaleyhouse.org

www.whitehouse.gov/ask/20031031-2.html

www.whitehouse.gov/history/life/video/index.html

www.winchestermysteryhouse.com

INDEX